We made this coloring Journal, to help you cope and relax your troubled mind. It's time to record your thoughts and color your way through. you are amazing!

MONTH AT A GLANCE

Habit Tracker

MONTH: _____

COLOR   ESSENTIAL HABITS

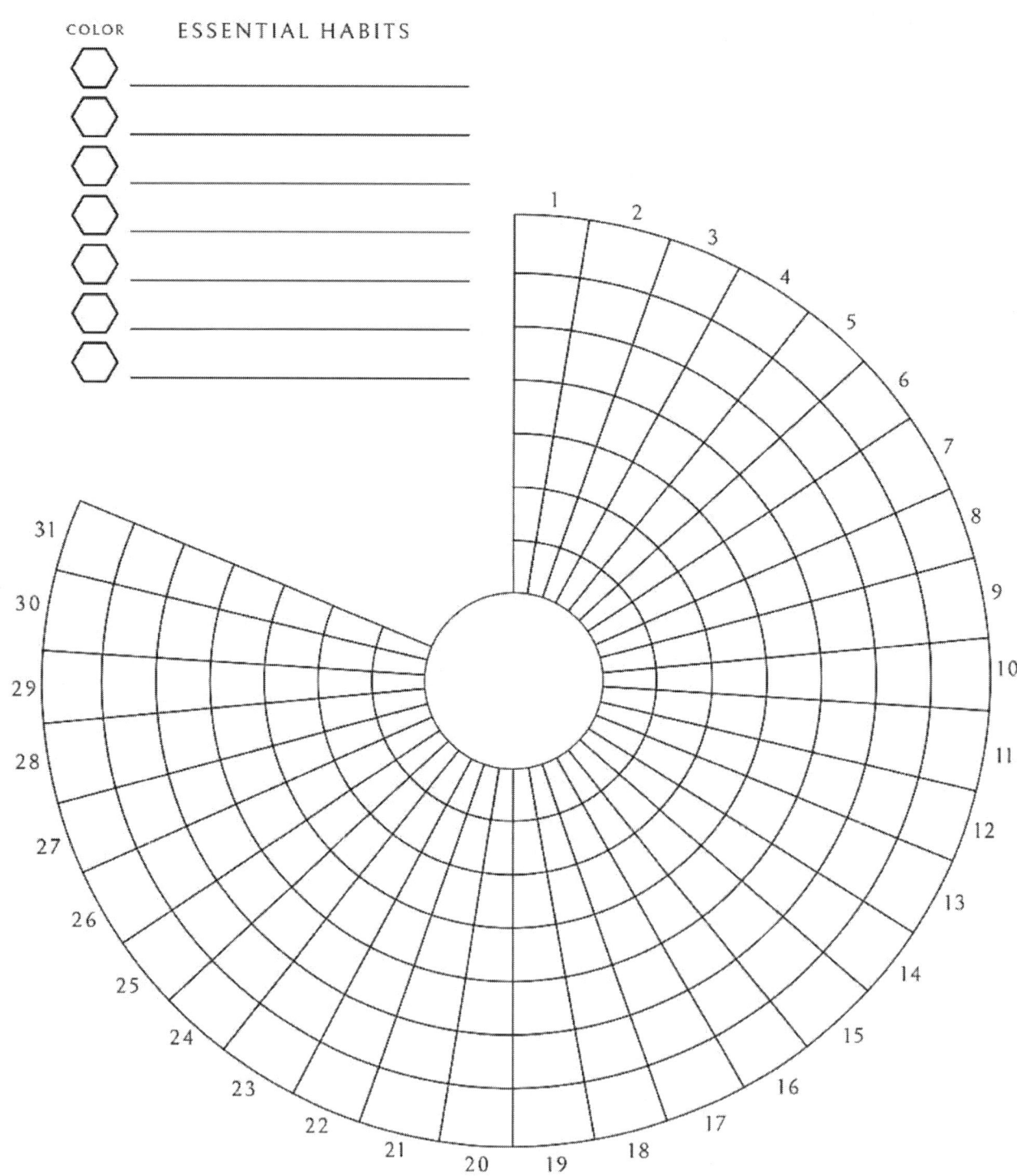

DATE : ....

> " My recovery must
> come first, so that
> everything i have
> in life does not
> have to come last.
> **ANONYMOUS**

DAYS SOBER

#

TODAY I FEEL : ....

TODAY I'M GRATEFUL FOR :

1 :

2 :

3 :

TODAY MY GOALS ARE:

....

....

....

MY MOOD TODAY :

WATER INTAKE :

TODAY I WILL SUPPORT MY

SOBRIETY
by doing
THIS **ONE** THING

THOUGHTS ABOUT TODAY

DATE : ....

I'm not telling you it is going to be easy; I'm telling you it's going to be worth it.

-ART WILLIAMS

DAYS SOBER

\#

TODAY I FEEL : ....

TODAY I'M GRATEFUL FOR :

1 :

2 :

3 :

TODAY MY GOALS ARE:

....

....

....

MY MOOD TODAY :

WATER INTAKE :

TODAY I WILL SUPPORT MY

SOBRIETY
by doing
THIS **ONE** THING

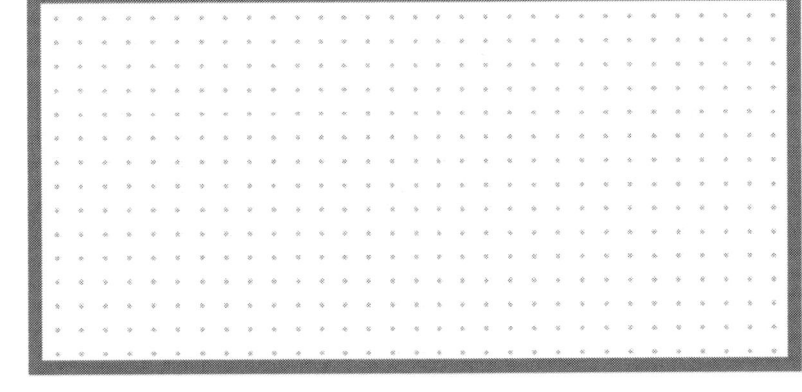

THOUGHTS ABOUT TODAY

DATE : ....

"Recovery didn't open the gates of heaven and let me in. Recovery opened the gates of hell and let me out"

-ANONYMOUS

DAYS SOBER

#

TODAY I FEEL : ....

TODAY I'M GRATEFUL FOR :

1 :

2 :

3 :

TODAY MY GOALS ARE:

....

....

....

MY MOOD TODAY :

WATER INTAKE :

TODAY I WILL SUPPORT MY SOBRIETY by doing THIS ONE THING

THOUGHTS ABOUT TODAY

DATE : ....

DAYS SOBER
#

TODAY I FEEL : ....

TODAY I'M GRATEFUL FOR :

1 :

2 :

3 :

TODAY MY GOALS ARE:

....

....

....

MY MOOD TODAY :

WATER INTAKE :

TODAY I WILL SUPPORT MY **SOBRIETY** *by doing* THIS **ONE** THING

THOUGHTS ABOUT TODAY

DATE : ....

"I understood myself only
after I destroyed myself. And
only in the process of fixing
myself, did I know who I
really was

**—SADE ANDRIA
ZABALA**

DAYS SOBER

#

TODAY I FEEL : ....

TODAY I'M GRATEFUL FOR :

1 :

2 :

3 :

TODAY MY GOALS ARE:

....

....

....

MY MOOD TODAY :

WATER INTAKE :

TODAY I WILL SUPPORT MY

SOBRIETY
by doing
THIS **ONE** THING

THOUGHTS ABOUT TODAY

DATE : ....

DAYS SOBER

#

> "The only person you are destined to become is the person you decide to be.

-RALPH WALDO EMERSON

TODAY I FEEL : ....

TODAY I'M GRATEFUL FOR :

1 :

2 :

3 :

TODAY MY GOALS ARE:

....

....

....

MY MOOD TODAY :

WATER INTAKE :

TODAY I WILL SUPPORT MY

SOBRIETY
by doing
THIS **ONE** THING

THOUGHTS ABOUT TODAY

DATE : ....

DAYS SOBER
#

"

TODAY I FEEL : ....

TODAY I'M GRATEFUL FOR :

1 :

2 :

3 :

TODAY MY GOALS ARE:

....

....

....

MY MOOD TODAY :

WATER INTAKE :

TODAY I WILL SUPPORT MY

SOBRIETY
by doing
THIS ONE THING

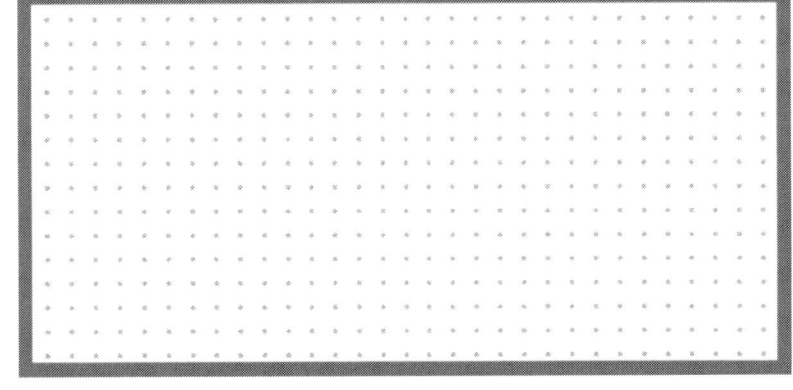

THOUGHTS ABOUT TODAY

DATE : ....

> All the suffering, stress, and addiction comes from not realizing you already are what you are looking for.
>
> **-JON KABAT-ZINN**

DAYS SOBER
#

TODAY I FEEL : ....

TODAY I'M GRATEFUL FOR :

1 :

2 :

3 :

TODAY MY GOALS ARE:

....

....

....

MY MOOD TODAY :

WATER INTAKE :

TODAY I WILL SUPPORT MY

SOBRIETY
by doing
THIS **ONE** THING

THOUGHTS ABOUT TODAY

DATE : ....

DAYS SOBER

#

TODAY I FEEL : ....

TODAY I'M GRATEFUL FOR :

1 :

2 :

3 :

TODAY MY GOALS ARE:

....

....

....

MY MOOD TODAY :

WATER INTAKE :

TODAY I WILL SUPPORT MY

SOBRIETY
by doing
THIS **ONE** THING

THOUGHTS ABOUT TODAY

DATE : ....

DAYS SOBER
#

"

TODAY I FEEL : ....

TODAY I'M GRATEFUL FOR :

1 :

2 :

3 :

TODAY MY GOALS ARE:

....

....

....

MY MOOD TODAY :

WATER INTAKE :

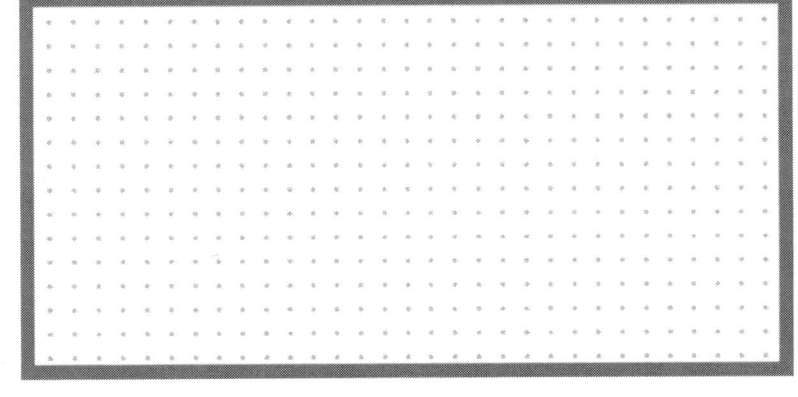

TODAY I WILL SUPPORT MY

SOBRIETY
by doing

THIS **ONE** THING

THOUGHTS ABOUT TODAY

DATE : ....

"
Recovery is not for people
who need it. It's for people
who want it.

-ANONYMOUS

DAYS SOBER

#

"

TODAY I FEEL : ....

TODAY I'M GRATEFUL FOR :

1 :

2 :

3 :

TODAY MY GOALS ARE:

....

....

....

MY MOOD TODAY :

WATER INTAKE :

TODAY I WILL SUPPORT MY

SOBRIETY
by doing
THIS ONE THING

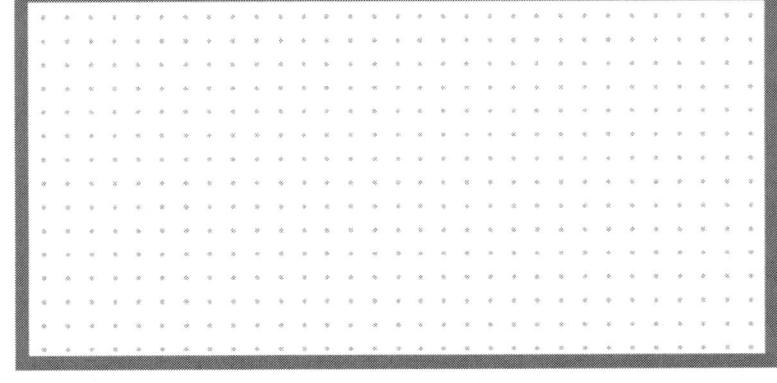

THOUGHTS ABOUT TODAY

DATE : ....

Nobody stays recovered **"** unless the life they have created is more rewarding and satisfying than the one they **"** left behind.

—ANNE FLETCHER

DAYS SOBER
#

TODAY I FEEL : ....

TODAY I'M GRATEFUL FOR :

1 :

2 :

3 :

TODAY MY GOALS ARE:

....

....

....

MY MOOD TODAY :

WATER INTAKE :

TODAY I WILL SUPPORT MY

SOBRIETY
by doing
THIS **ONE** THING

THOUGHTS ABOUT TODAY

DATE : ....

"I am not defined by my relapses, but by my decision to remain in recovery despite them"

— ANONYMOUS

DAYS SOBER
#

TODAY I FEEL : ....

TODAY I'M GRATEFUL FOR :

1 :

2 :

3 :

TODAY MY GOALS ARE:

....

....

....

MY MOOD TODAY :

WATER INTAKE :

TODAY I WILL SUPPORT MY
SOBRIETY
by doing
THIS **ONE** THING

THOUGHTS ABOUT TODAY

DATE : ....

"There is no shame in beginning again, for you get a chance to build bigger and better than before.

-LEON BROWN

DAYS SOBER

#

TODAY I FEEL : ....

TODAY I'M GRATEFUL FOR :

1 :

2 :

3 :

TODAY MY GOALS ARE:

....

....

....

MY MOOD TODAY :

WATER INTAKE :

TODAY I WILL SUPPORT MY

SOBRIETY
by doing

THIS ONE THING

THOUGHTS ABOUT TODAY

DATE : ....

DAYS SOBER
#

"

Relapses are almost an inevitable part of any course of self-development.

-PHILLIPA PERRY

"

TODAY I FEEL : ....

TODAY I'M GRATEFUL FOR :

1 :

2 :

3 :

TODAY MY GOALS ARE:

....

....

....

MY MOOD TODAY :

WATER INTAKE :

TODAY I WILL SUPPORT MY

SOBRIETY
by doing
THIS **ONE** THING

THOUGHTS ABOUT TODAY

DATE : ....

"Part of recovery is relapse. I dust myself off and move forward again.

" **—STEVEN ALDER**

DAYS SOBER

#

TODAY I FEEL : ....

TODAY I'M GRATEFUL FOR :

1 :

2 :

3 :

TODAY MY GOALS ARE:

....

....

....

MY MOOD TODAY :

WATER INTAKE :

TODAY I WILL SUPPORT MY

SOBRIETY *by doing* THIS **ONE** THING

THOUGHTS ABOUT TODAY

DATE : ....

There's no such thing as quitting. Just sometimes, there's a long pause between relapses.

"

— ALAN MOORE

DAYS SOBER
#

TODAY I FEEL : ....

TODAY I'M GRATEFUL FOR :

1 :

2 :

3 :

TODAY MY GOALS ARE:

....

....

....

MY MOOD TODAY :

WATER INTAKE :

TODAY I WILL SUPPORT MY

SOBRIETY
by doing
THIS **ONE** THING

THOUGHTS ABOUT TODAY

DATE : ....

DAYS SOBER

#

> Recovery is taking all twelve steps...over and over and over and over...

– TONI SORENSON

TODAY I FEEL : ....

TODAY I'M GRATEFUL FOR :

1 :

2 :

3 :

TODAY MY GOALS ARE:

....

....

....

MY MOOD TODAY :

WATER INTAKE :

TODAY I WILL SUPPORT MY

SOBRIETY
by doing
THIS ONE THING

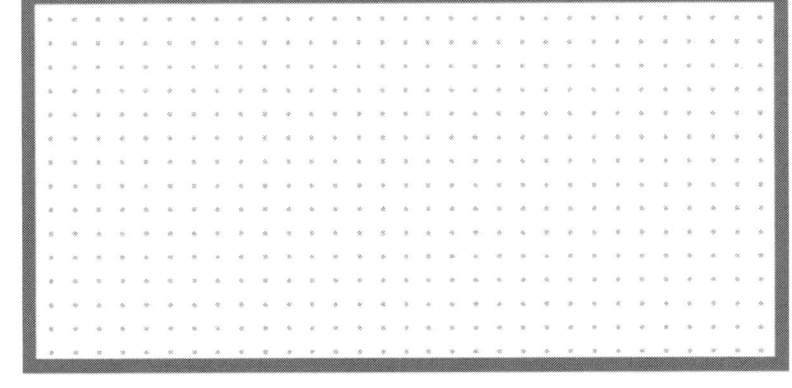

THOUGHTS ABOUT TODAY

DATE : ....

> Recovery is not a race. You don't have to feel guilty if it takes you longer than you thought it would.
>
> — UNKNOWN

DAYS SOBER

#

TODAY I FEEL : ....

TODAY I'M GRATEFUL FOR :

1 :

2 :

3 :

TODAY MY GOALS ARE:

....

....

....

MY MOOD TODAY :

WATER INTAKE :

TODAY I WILL SUPPORT MY SOBRIETY by doing THIS ONE THING

THOUGHTS ABOUT TODAY

DATE : ....

> The man who moves a mountain begins by carrying away small stones.
>
> — CONFUCIUS

DAYS SOBER

#

TODAY I FEEL : ....

TODAY I'M GRATEFUL FOR :

1 :

2 :

3 :

TODAY MY GOALS ARE:

....

....

....

MY MOOD TODAY :

WATER INTAKE :

TODAY I WILL SUPPORT MY SOBRIETY by doing THIS ONE THING

THOUGHTS ABOUT TODAY

DATE : ....

> "Recovery is something you have to work on every single day, and it's something that doesn't get a day off."
> — DEMI LOVATO

DAYS SOBER
# #

TODAY I FEEL : ....

TODAY I'M GRATEFUL FOR :

1 :
2 :
3 :

TODAY MY GOALS ARE:

....

....

....

MY MOOD TODAY :

WATER INTAKE :

TODAY I WILL SUPPORT MY
SOBRIETY
by doing
THIS ONE THING

THOUGHTS ABOUT TODAY

DATE : ....

> One thing you must realize is that: you either kill your addiction or your addiction will eventually kill you.
>
> — OCHE OTORKPA

DAYS SOBER #

TODAY I FEEL : ....

TODAY I'M GRATEFUL FOR :

1 :
2 :
3 :

TODAY MY GOALS ARE:

....

....

....

MY MOOD TODAY :

WATER INTAKE :

TODAY I WILL SUPPORT MY SOBRIETY by doing THIS ONE THING

THOUGHTS ABOUT TODAY

DATE : ....

DAYS SOBER
#

> We should be open to change to ensure that our addiction to life always remains under check.

— DR. PREM JAGYASI

TODAY I FEEL : ....

TODAY I'M GRATEFUL FOR :

1 :

2 :

3 :

TODAY MY GOALS ARE:

....

....

....

MY MOOD TODAY :

WATER INTAKE :

TODAY I WILL SUPPORT MY
SOBRIETY
by doing
THIS ONE THING

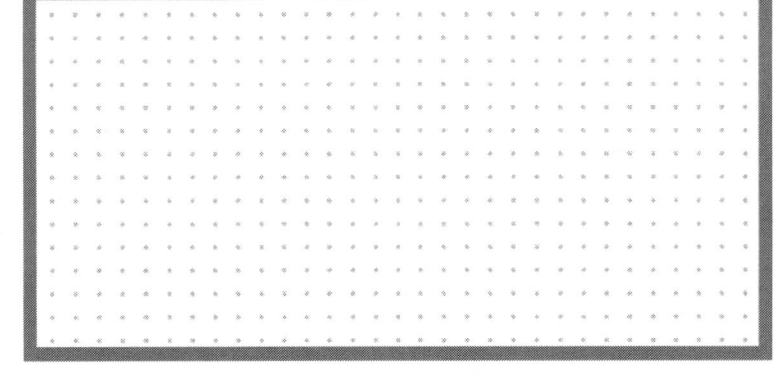

THOUGHTS ABOUT TODAY

DATE : ....

DAYS SOBER
#

TODAY I FEEL : ....

TODAY I'M GRATEFUL FOR :

1 :

2 :

3 :

TODAY MY GOALS ARE:

....

....

....

MY MOOD TODAY :

WATER INTAKE :

TODAY I WILL SUPPORT MY

SOBRIETY
by doing
THIS **ONE** THING

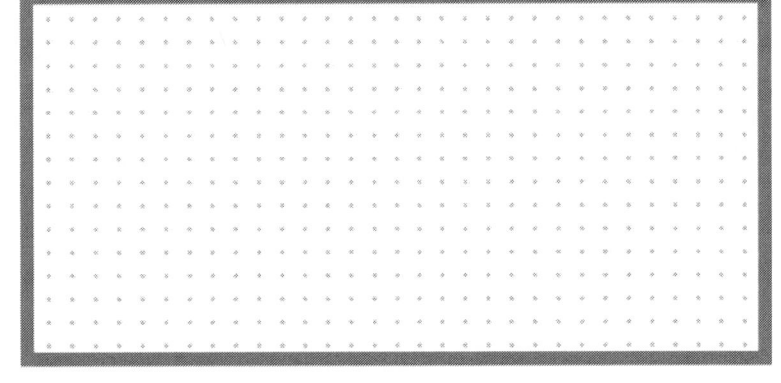

THOUGHTS ABOUT TODAY

DATE : ....

> "Your addiction is not you, but it feels like you because you've spent so much intimate time together"
>
> — TONI SORENSON

DAYS SOBER
#

TODAY I FEEL : ....

TODAY I'M GRATEFUL FOR :

1 :

2 :

3 :

TODAY MY GOALS ARE:

....

....

....

MY MOOD TODAY :

WATER INTAKE :

TODAY I WILL SUPPORT MY
SOBRIETY
by doing
THIS ONE THING

THOUGHTS ABOUT TODAY

DATE : ....

DAYS SOBER
#

TODAY I FEEL : ....

TODAY I'M GRATEFUL FOR :

1 :

2 :

3 :

TODAY MY GOALS ARE:

....

....

....

MY MOOD TODAY :

WATER INTAKE :

TODAY I WILL SUPPORT MY

SOBRIETY
by doing
THIS **ONE** THING

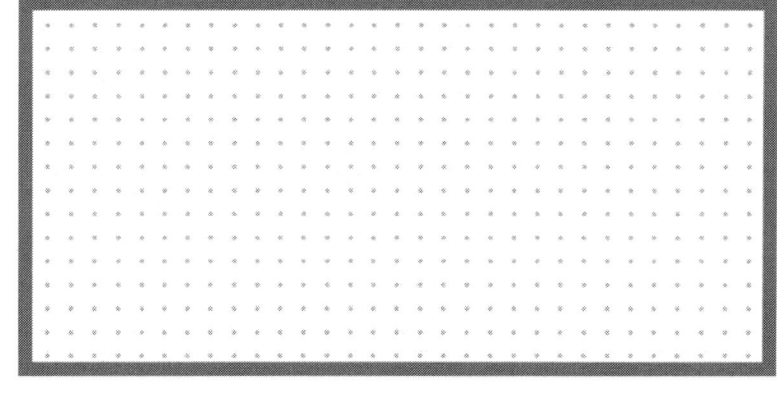

THOUGHTS ABOUT TODAY

DATE : ....

DAYS SOBER
#

TODAY I FEEL : ....

TODAY I'M GRATEFUL FOR :

1 :

2 :

3 :

TODAY MY GOALS ARE:

....

....

....

MY MOOD TODAY :

WATER INTAKE :

TODAY I WILL SUPPORT MY
SOBRIETY
by doing
THIS ONE THING

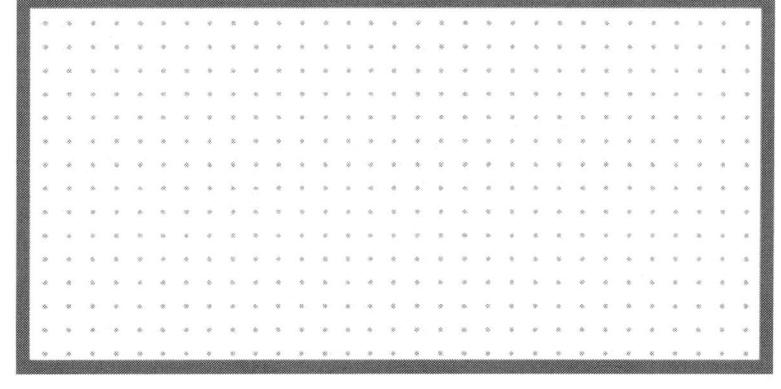

THOUGHTS ABOUT TODAY

DATE : ....

DAYS SOBER

#

TODAY I FEEL : ....

TODAY I'M GRATEFUL FOR :

1 :

2 :

3 :

TODAY MY GOALS ARE:

....

....

....

MY MOOD TODAY :

WATER INTAKE :

TODAY I WILL SUPPORT MY

SOBRIETY
by doing
THIS **ONE** THING

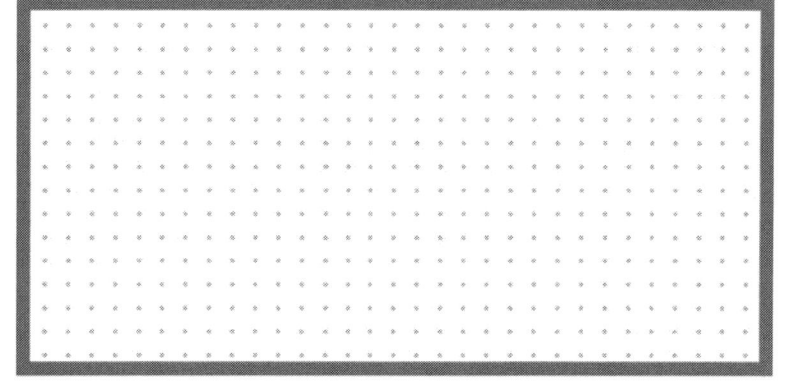

THOUGHTS ABOUT TODAY

DATE : ....

DAYS SOBER

#

TODAY I FEEL : ....

TODAY I'M GRATEFUL FOR :

1 :

2 :

3 :

TODAY MY GOALS ARE:

....

....

....

MY MOOD TODAY :

WATER INTAKE :

TODAY I WILL SUPPORT MY SOBRIETY by doing THIS ONE THING

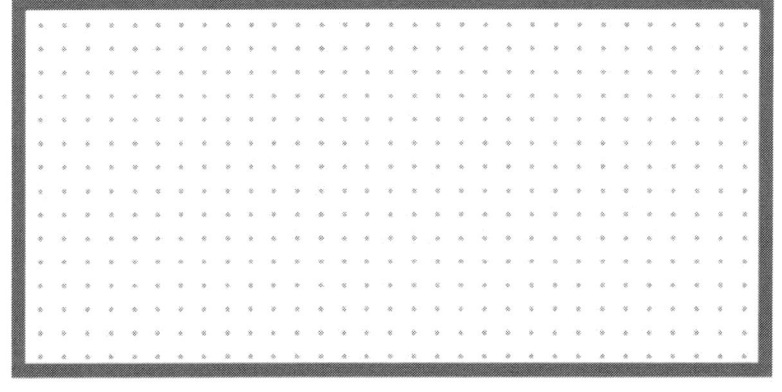

THOUGHTS ABOUT TODAY

DATE : ....

DAYS SOBER #

> "People often say motivation doesn't last. Neither does bathing—that's why we recommend it daily."
>
> **—ZIG ZIGLAR**

TODAY I FEEL : ....

TODAY I'M GRATEFUL FOR :

1 :

2 :

3 :

TODAY MY GOALS ARE:

....

....

....

MY MOOD TODAY :

WATER INTAKE :

TODAY I WILL SUPPORT MY **SOBRIETY** *by doing* THIS **ONE** THING

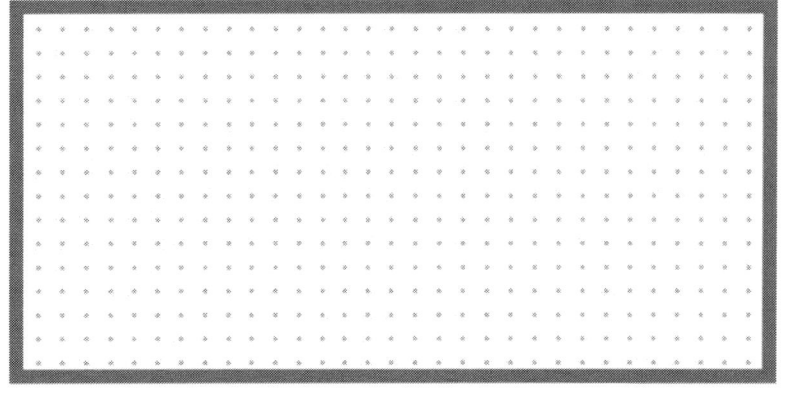

THOUGHTS ABOUT TODAY

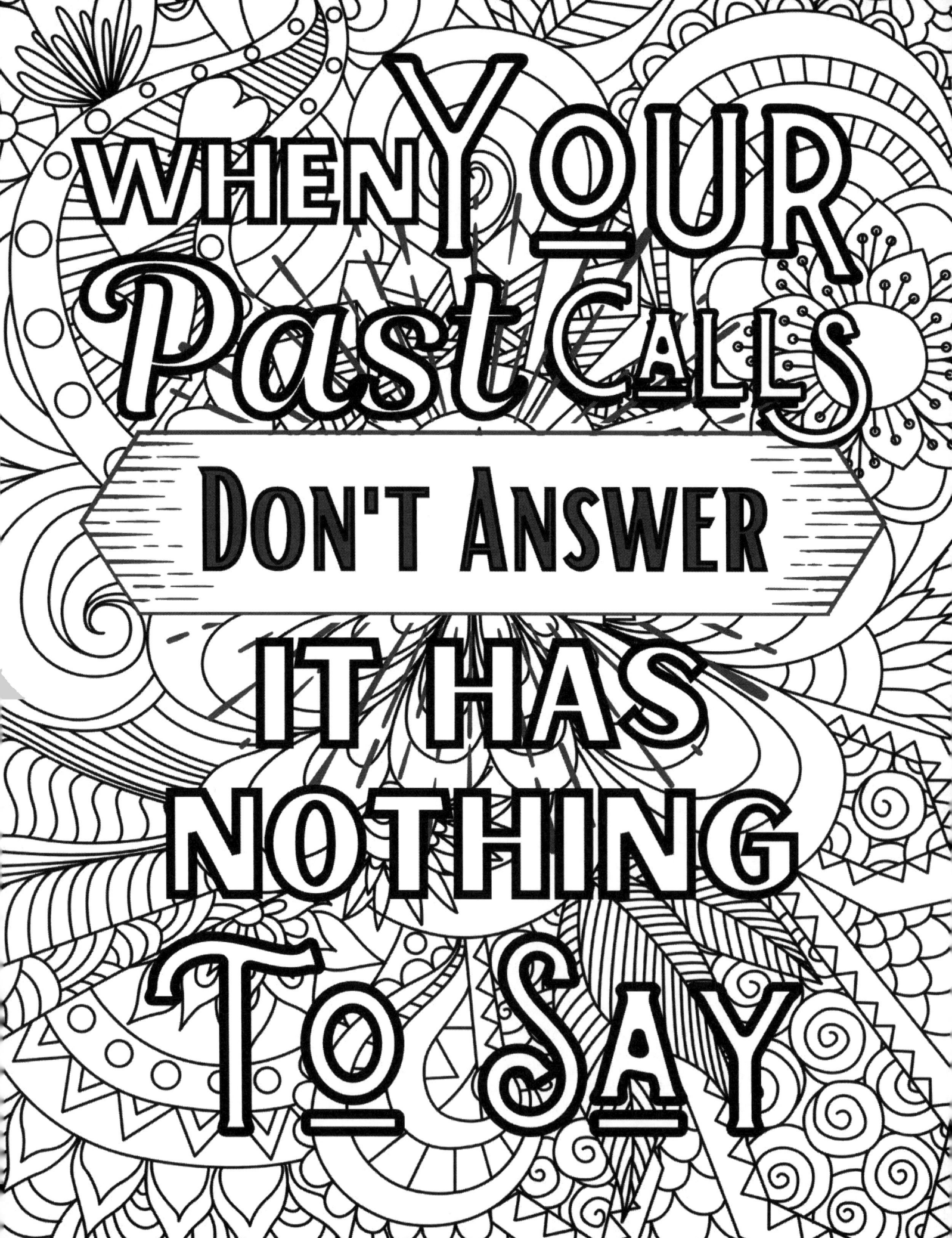

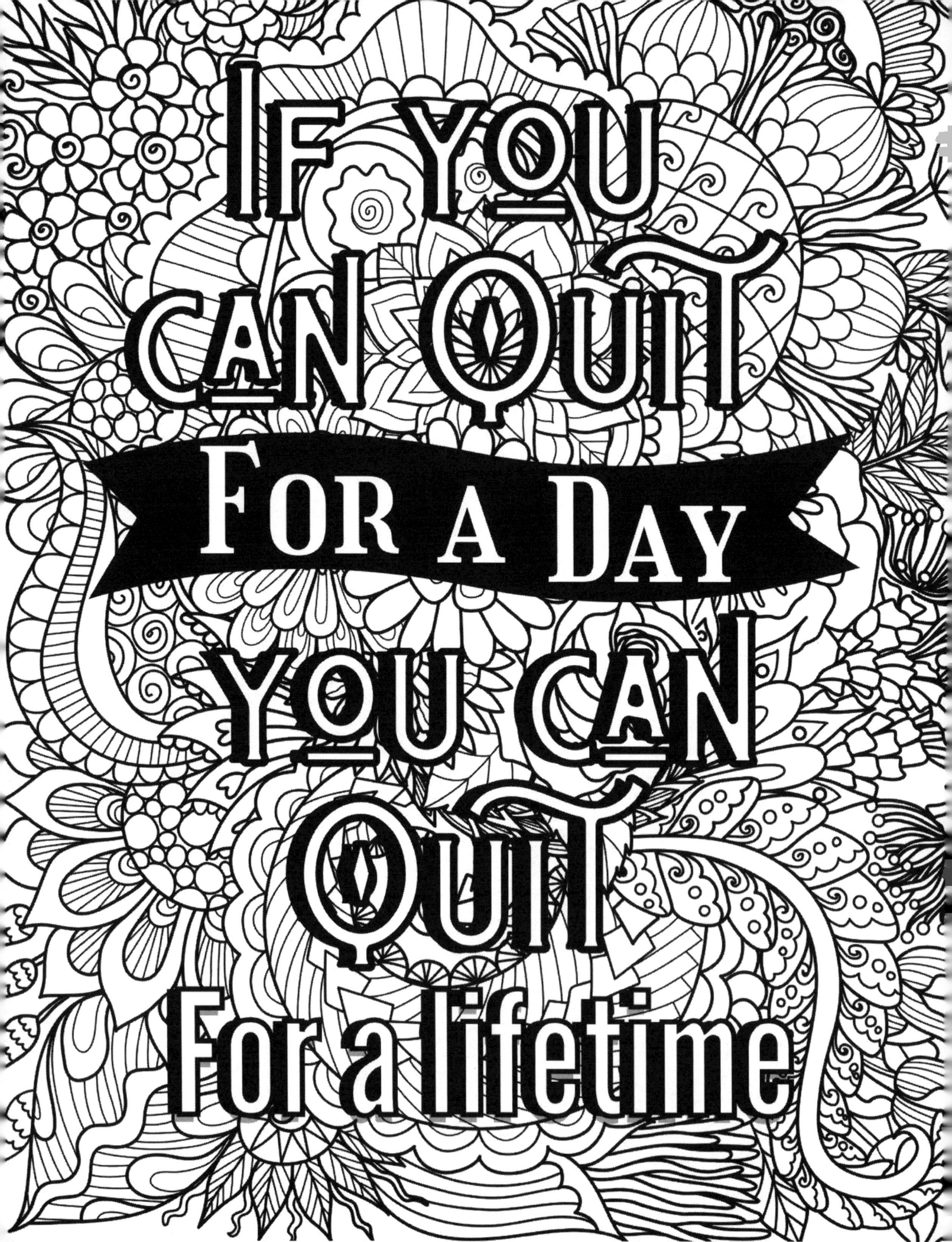

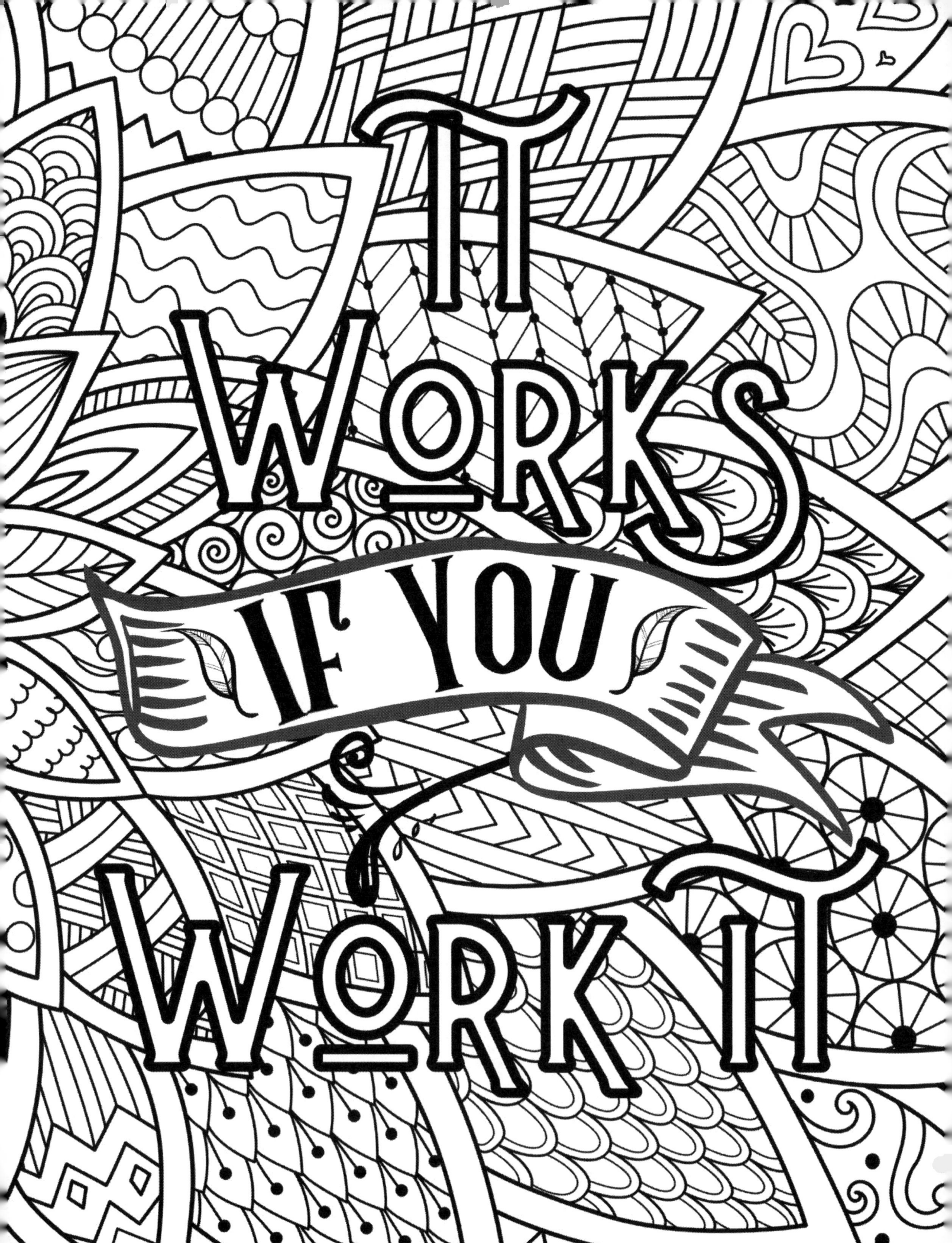

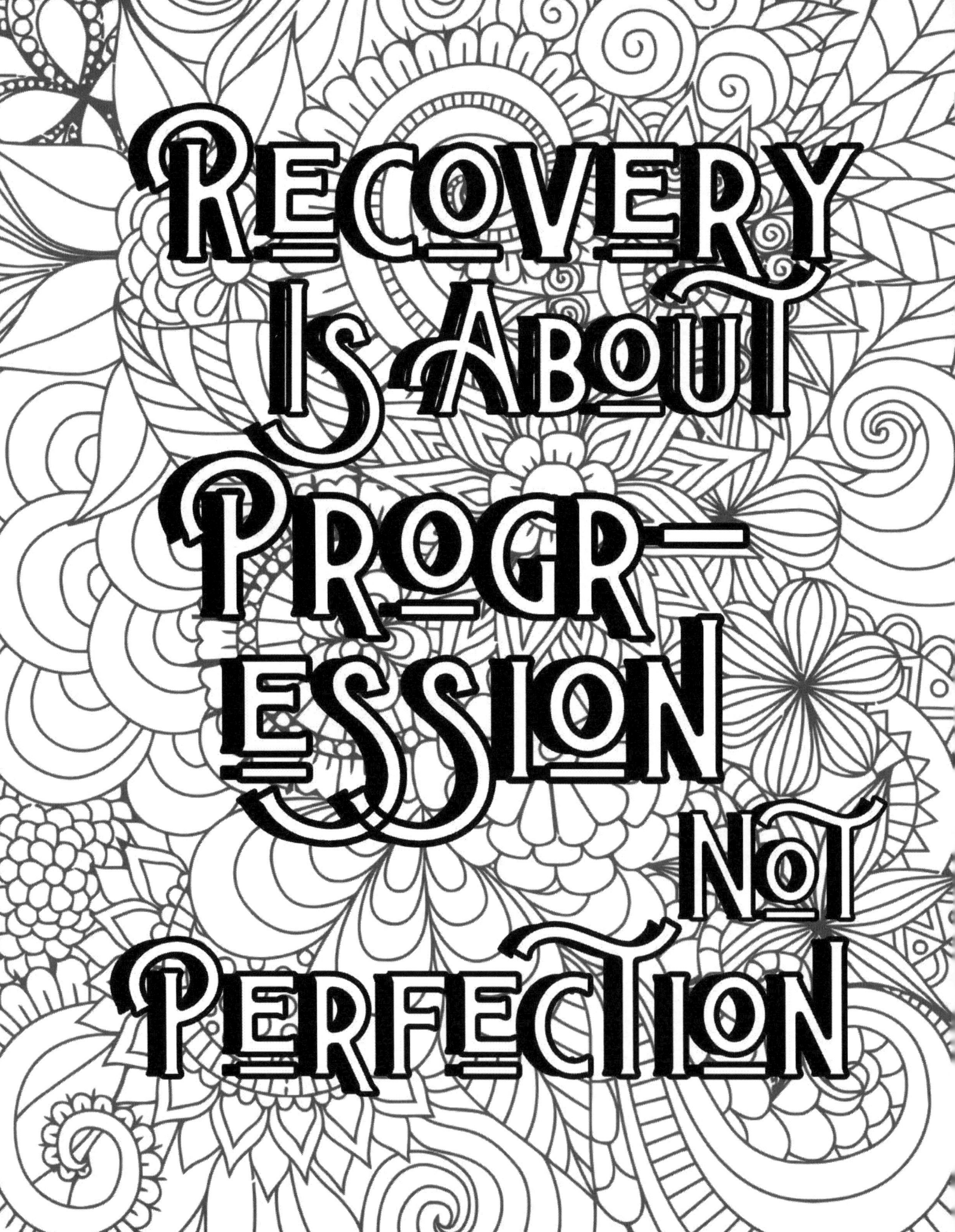

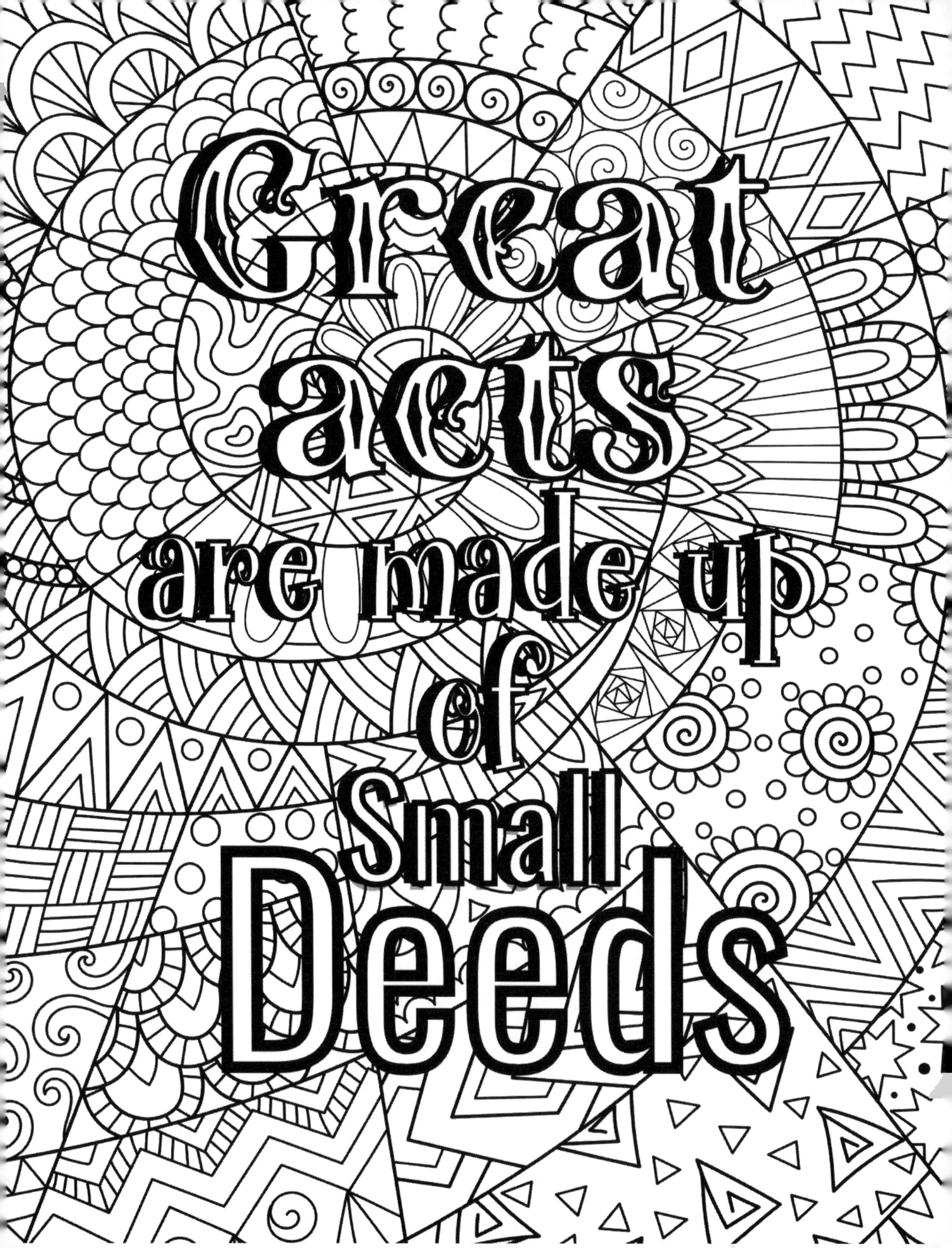

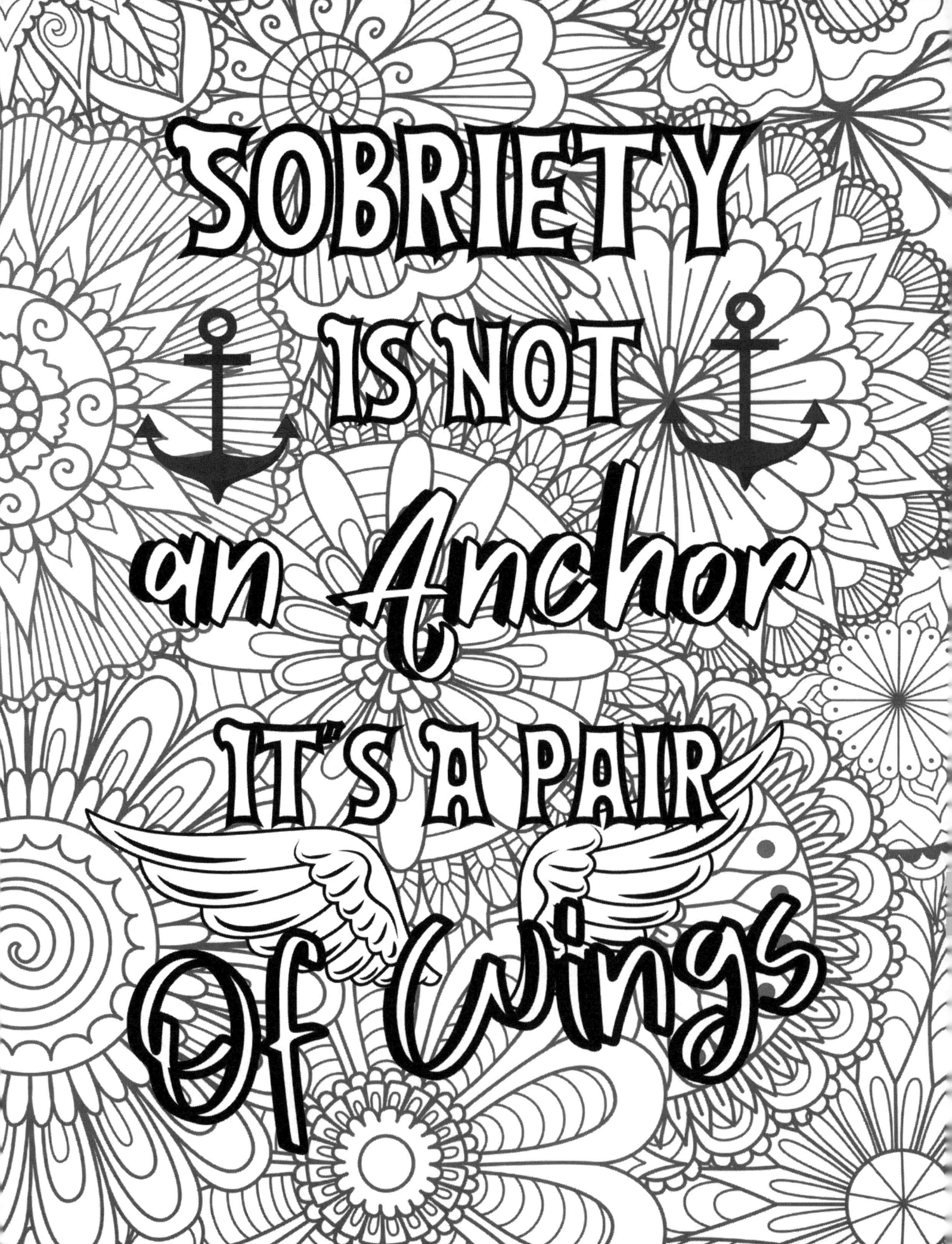

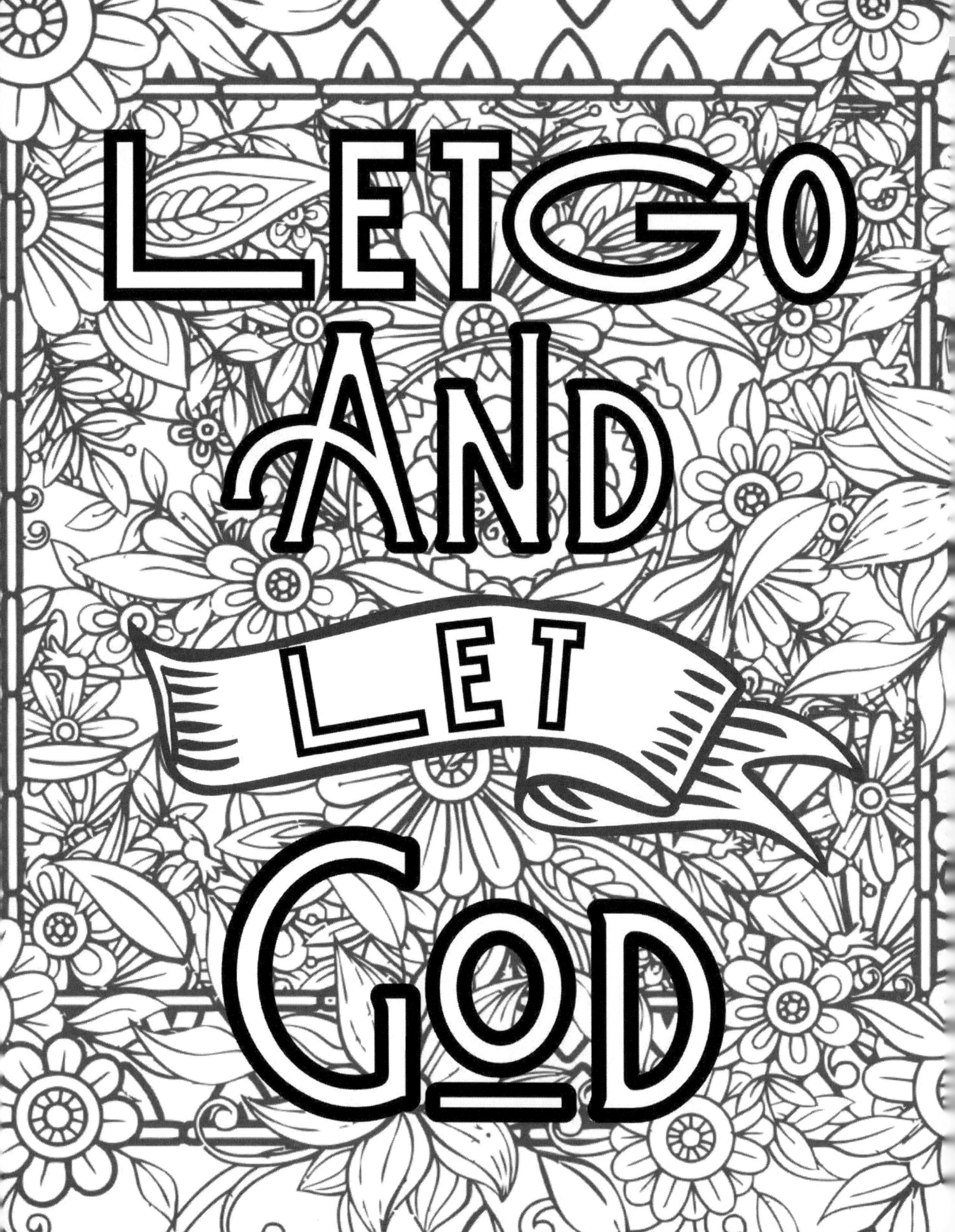

SPECIAL REQUEST

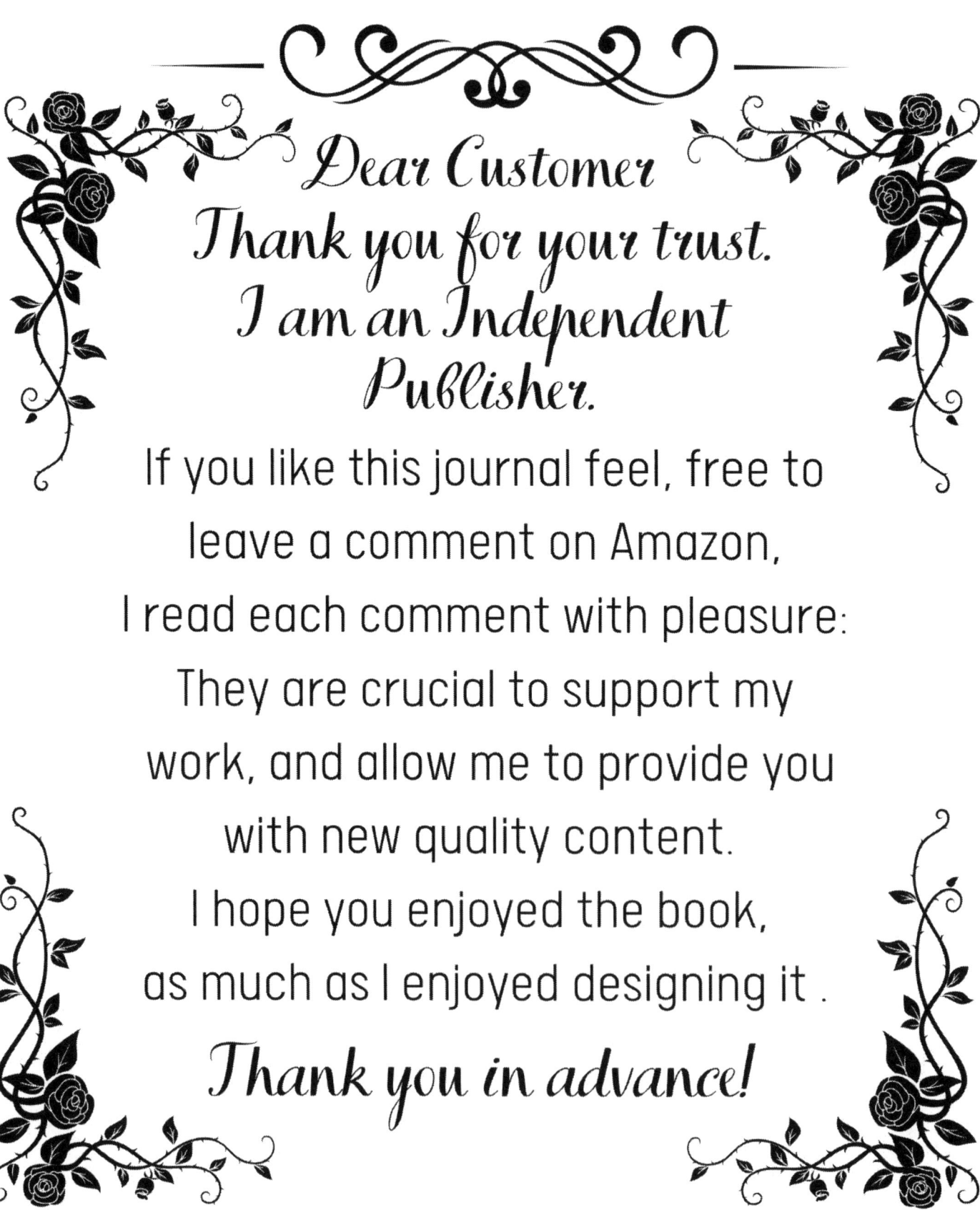

Dear Customer
Thank you for your trust.
I am an Independent
Publisher.

If you like this journal feel, free to
leave a comment on Amazon,
I read each comment with pleasure:
They are crucial to support my
work, and allow me to provide you
with new quality content.
I hope you enjoyed the book,
as much as I enjoyed designing it .

Thank you in advance!

Manufactured by Amazon.ca
Bolton, ON